The Harvest

Ever do we turn the earth, like gods turning souls,
old sun turning vigorous dark.... Where steel teeth
sever the soil, led out under night, gaunt workers
strike the ground, to serenade howling vultures.

Bacterial tangles huddle in a mother's smother; hang,
as metal blades slice earth and through the morning.
In the haggle, thrash and rot, ammonia clusters bleed.
Rain charms the oath; the mortal angel. Seedlings bud.

Voices range beyond the hills.
Birdsong echoes in the valley.

Acidulated soil shifts to rites and crops,
edaphic distillations of assorted crust.
Of sacred soil, the arid sun-disc tilts atop;
an aspect of Osiris clouds the tidal dirts,
to drop so, in the delta's sacrificial dusts.

When medieval scribes give the Angel of Death a scythe,
the white doves gather. Mad Heaven begs a life in cycles;
the harvest of a glitch in seeds — a gem evinced by a wheel.

Voices range beyond the hills.
Birdsong echoes in the valley.

Fertile territory sits on picketed hills. A plough
rolls in the dirt, like the corpse of a guilty priest.
Poetic Sky has let, or spilt, her glitter in our field.
Flora rot. Her pirouetting sickle splits the yield.

Nature reaps but grief in hillside crypts. Although I trek,
rough scriptures dig the flesh, abrupt eternity, in alkali.
Further up, beside that court, the granary is spilling like
a punctured hourglass — a thresher tilting, brief like pity.

Voices range beyond the hills.
Birdsong echoes in the valley.

The fatal yeomen sigh gravestones
of air to the glassy heavens. Men get
to fight one angel every mass. As the
grains then go heave to leafy stems,
those same early evening fogs that
soften the years save the gloaming.
Gone to mists, feathery leaves hang
in the heavy, agglomerate softness....

Voices range beyond the hills.
Birdsong echoes in the valley.

Those plough blades rise and set in early wreaths,
to shade the barley's wail, this reaper's golden sun....
Uphill, the oats are sown and gather eyeless birds.

The reaping is
in their pages.

We harrow grit and free a sun, in
fear — a wraith renewing rounds.
We are grains and in the furrow.

Voices range beyond the hills.
Birdsong echoes in the valley.

Chaos and the Furrows

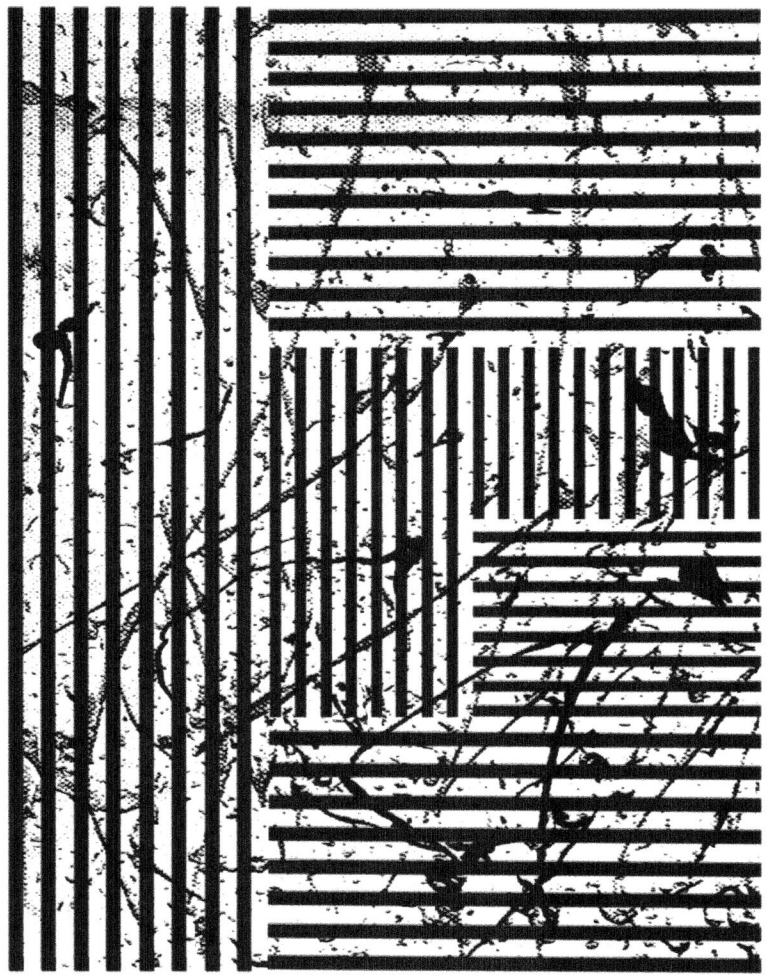

ATOMS, GODS AND THE VOID

Metamorphoses

ARTEMIS AND DIANA

Wars I met,
raw as trade,
reflip an aid.
I drowse; I raid....
       Sumer's a weld:
       Arcadia's stir
       (we wake, ergo, troop still...).
              A dewy Rome,
              made muse,
              rose to note,
              so resumed a memory;
              wed all its poor
              to Greek awe.
Writs said a cradle was Remus,
diaries' word.
       I, Diana, pilfered:
       art saw Artemis raw.

APOLLO AND ARTEMIS

Apollo and Artemis
map rational Delos:
     Rome adopts all in a
     pastoral, in a model.
     It plans a moral ode
     and pools material.
          In drama's pale loot,
          a Latin dream loops,
          to roam, spell Diana —
          a pallid moon's tear....

APOLLO ELEVEN

In fallen atoms, poets' arms,
soon, Artemis plants flame....
     A planet rests, films a moon,
     Apollo's men (faint masters):
     It's one small step for a man —
     man's leap for a stolen mist.

Labyrinths

MINOS

Daedalus, nine pass.
I, Minos, add a son....
I miss a peninsula, dead.

THESEUS AND ARIADNE

Spool's end: Air, an isle.
Vary. A way ravels in
Ariadne's loops.

THE MINOTAUR

The mythical sun faded, Borges' Asterion
softly dies.... The aged Minotaur branches,
bred, as unity names the logic of threads.
        Hybrid asterisms don the cult of Aegean
        myth: Ariadne's corona. Theseus' bled gift.

Siege of Troy

PARIS AND MENELAUS

Sir, a prism or feud?
Raw deed — in a trap, say?
      Menelaus: A casual enemy, a Spartan.
      I deed war, due from Sir Paris.

ILIAD AND AENEID

Do glare far:
Aeneid nets Iliad.
      Negate, spar, Troy!
      A siege, I say, or trap set.
         Agenda:
         I listen;
         die near a feral god.

ROME REBUILDS

      The Iliad courses ageless noblewoman Helen of Sparta.
(See sage Menelaus fashion blood on lips, the claret war!)
      Long oats of the Hellenic pass saw Rome rebuild Aeneas.
(See Paris battle Achilles — shown under a moon of eagles!)
      All fiction breathes a shadow on our lenses, peels a gem:
The Aeneid lulls, warps Greece's atoms — in a halo of bones.

The Perseids

HERACLES' LABOURS

In Heracles' Labours:
Cerberus' lash. A lion.
A bull. Heroic snares.
His nebular oracles....

HERACLES THE PERSEID

So gradual dies repose, tale,
drowsy metal lets no cities pale.
     So, Leo frets.
     No more hydra.
     Heracles, seven in....
          A canine vessel?
          Care, hardy hero! Monster foe!
          Lose, lapse it!
               I constellate my sword, elate.
               So, Perseid, laud Argos.

THE PERSEID METEORS

Perseid — a meteor shower muddling sagas —
wields Gorgon Medusa's stare. He primed a
shield, demigod Perseus; wrote anagrams
in gem-stars. He rode Pegasus, roamed wild,
promised Andromeda surges with eagles....

Theogony

COSMOGONIES

From Hesiod's cosmogony, be a true primeval sky:
forms like Ovid's, by our agency — metamorphoses,
my void. Chaos gestures broken memory, a slip of
dark nebulae. My cosmos promises the ivory fog....

TITANOMACHIES

Titanomachies!
   A mist inchoate.
   The actions aim
   a theistic moan —
      It's in each atom:
      Intimate Chaos.

ZEUS AND OLYMPUS

So: Ah, Cronus!
We name open Olympus, aware still a deity rots onsite.
  My Mnemosyne! Go next, far.
  Cognise. Resume:
  No Muses lessen a Titan, a Titaness, else sum one Muse.
    Resin, go craft xenogeny, so men.
      My Metis: no story tied all.
      Its era was up —
      my lone poem
      a new sun
      or Chaos.

The Atomists

CLINAMEN

A mix.
A myriad I overused.
A maybe decimal set.
A lamina, forever of anima.
  Late slam!
  I cede — by a made, sure void — airy maxima.

LEUCIPPUS AND DEMOCRITUS

Leucippus and Democritus:
I curl up, atomic, suspended
in space's pure-to-lucid mud.
Nuclei add up time's corpus....
Epics, duplicated, mourn us:
Cupid, and Lucretius' poems;
Epicurus' sculpted domain....

NUCLEOSYNTHESIS

Spaces ago, here in nebulosity,
echoes gain issuable entropy,
inspire theogony's able cause:
each pulse into baryogenesis.
(Chaos rises on, peeling beauty....)
I probe age, nucleosynthesis;
course enthalpy, abiogenesis;
encourage pale biosynthesis,
hissing poetry, a sea once blue....

Prometheus and His Creation

SACRED
NUMBERS

Ratio (Aelindrome in φ)

16180339887498948482

Old, rational ways gleam
pictures I coil and frame
in detained
theorems
and in the new score.

In space,
read the worth;
read vines now as lines.

Now a sad view or thread,
thin space renews cores
and,
in the ore, mined.

Theme in detail
and fractures, I compile
an always-gold ratio....

Matrix (Aelindrome in √2)

14142135623730950488

Matrix:
In deal,
in omen,
abide, deep with me.

Log
arithmetic.
Go early.
Kind estimates
move approximates.

Modestly kinetic, go earth me.

Logarithm wide,
deepen
a binomial
index,
a trim....

Asymptote (Aelindrome in e)

27182818284590452353

Infinite sets,
to unity,
present critical
enterprises,
over a map.

Ether, I eat ash.

To me,
asymptotic log is key,
logistic to a symptom,
eerie, at a shape....

The ramp-rise
(so vertical, entire)
sent crypts
to unite
finites in.

Geometry (Aelindrome in π)

31415926535897932384

I nest a cone;
index angles in veer —
a concave,
penta-tangential
in a pit.

Hypotenuse up,
we closet here
phrase or line,
a plane,
or (linear) a sphere....

We close, then use up,
a pithy potential,
in a tangent cave,
per a convex angle.

Sine: indent a cosine....

Piaelindromes

<u>THE SECTOR</u>
314159

Spiral tears are
cut.
A sector's area alters:
Pi.

<u>THE SOLSTICE</u>
3141592653589

Solstice:
New, it evokes
old needs
and raw senses.
>Sun rids us.
>What binds us bids us.
>What sunrise saw
>sends and reevokes.
>Old, new...
>it entices Sol.

Prime Aelindromes

<u>CHAINS</u>
235723572357

Aside,
a dour death
remains
in changes....
Archival
prime numbers
(primeval hinges)
arc in chains
made a thread:
our ideas.

<u>SOLAR ECLIPSE, LUNAR ECLIPSE</u>
235723572357

On smoky earth
is dark's mar
of tender Gaia
or distant omens....
      A titan,
      to disorder,
      Gaia
      often marks
      this
      dark
      year's Moon....

Visual Aelindrome in e

27182818284590452353

THE LILITH
SONNETS

Eyes of Horus

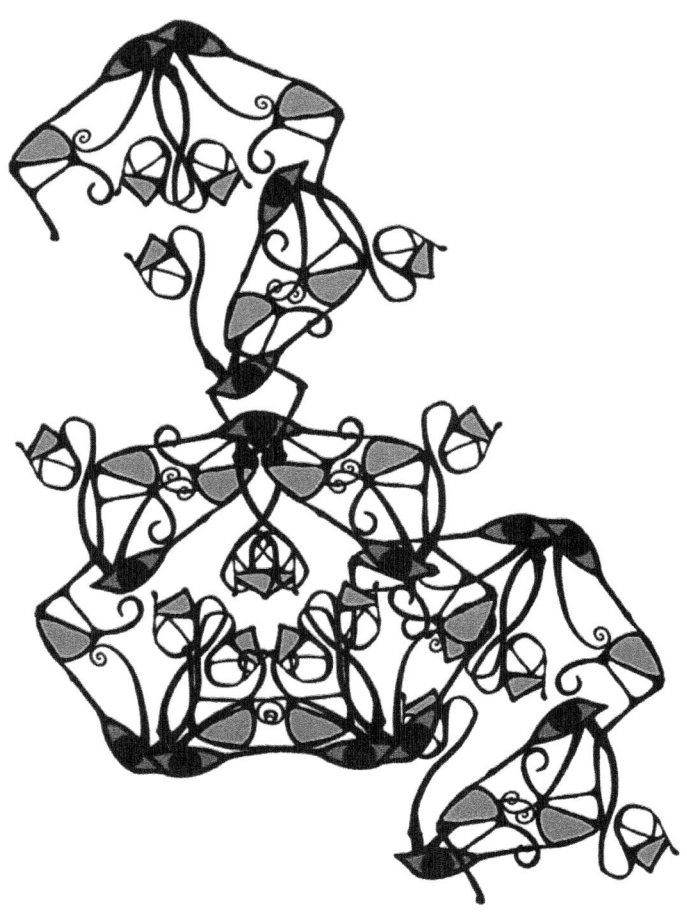

Lilith and Hecate

I stirred, there, cups of haemoglobin. True.
There's magic in our blood, the purest fire.
The nighttime pours a red, or cries of blue;
bright Luna comes to pour the rife desire....

Horrific, gruesome battles (hope untried)
are fought, remote, in scriptures I behold.
The rip or turn of loss became their guide:
"Rise up!" The rust of iron became their gold.

From Hecate rebuilt, their grip's due soon.
Before she put their drum to Grecian soil,
I buried starlight, sure creep of the Moon;

demure of air, I brought the serpent's coil.
Rebuild me too! Repair the curse of nights —
before I rule, through past demonic rites!

Lilith and Pan

Name, by a mark's, a *minus deus* sign.
I snap, sir. I so set a coven robe.
Regard: A bone rips. Stars do, grey, align.
O, madness, end a bond I buoy, to probe.

Writs damn a gap, a gnostic at no mood.
Gold net, tail adepts. All abet a nest.
Act set, an olive deviant, I brood —
do orbit, naïve devil, on a test.

Cat senate: Ballast, pedal, I attend.
Log doom, on tacit song, a pagan mad.
(Stir web or pot, you bid no badness end.)

Among, I layer gods.... Rats spire no bad.
Rage, reborn, evocates Osiris, Pan.
Sing, issued sun! I mask Ra — maybe man.

Lilith and Ra

A demon eel stays cradled. Pen out youth.
My! Add bled sun, so read tense idols soon.
Moat: gods burn. How that stir of trance is truth!
Desire its witch art over all. Be noon.

In Ra, add, so oblige, paganic songs.
All pets as acts, hill fawn, do phrase it slow.
Anubis, gold Ra, heed a theme — heat long.
Wit owing, loathe me: "Heated herald, go!"

I sub a now-slit seraph. Downfall hits.
A cast spell sang, so I can age. (Pig blood's
a drain — on no bell, rave, to arch its wit....)

Reside thru Stein. Craft rot, its hawthorn buds.
Goat-Moon! Sol's doe instead resounds, led bad.
Myth out, you end; plead, "Crystal, see one mad!"

Lilith and Hades

"Rise, Lilith, see above the burning light!"
Skies hollow into empty, bleeding clouds.
Death purest, the revenge of weary night,
draws Hades where, below, the answer shrouds.

Breath steady, her resolve to follow snakes
roars measures she demands to ever hold:
Cold visions in opaque and fiery lakes;
lakes, fiery and opaque in visions cold.

"Hold ever to demands!" She measures roars.
Snakes follow, to resolve her steady breath.
Shrouds answer the Below, where Hades draws.

Night weary of revenge, the purest death;
clouds bleeding empty, into hollow skies;
light burning the Above — see Lilith rise!

Lilith and Enlil

In bloody dreams,
the gods enlist
exotic screams
whose fires persist
in quartz.... The mist
that Enlil swirled
and Lilith hissed,
this way, unfurled
the underworld —
Ereshkigal,
a serpent curled
within her skull,
is conjured there,
in larval prayer....

Alchemy

WEAPONS OF WAR

Arrows and Bows

ONE

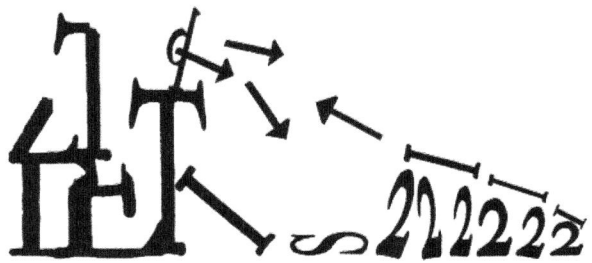

Steel felt sacred.
Lower, get a flat,
Roman Iron Age bow to draw.
Foster ruts, as turrets of war do.
Two began, or, in a mortal fate,
grew older:
Castle, fleets....

Sheath,
on its perch.
Arrow and tail.
A tempo to owe bones on stones.
One bow-to-poem, atilt,
and war —
O, archer, spit on the ash.

Its trap,
or form, is torn,
as rains issue its arrows.
In bows, in rows,
are its suns.
I rain —
a storm is for portraits.

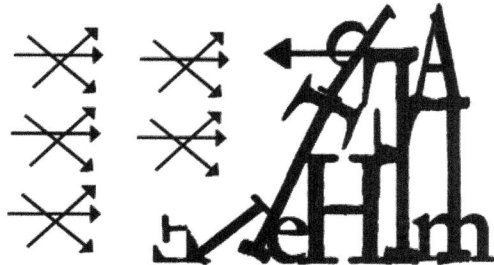

Castles shell rows,
near my lost instructor.
Sever verse, per the covetous omen.
Bow, metal bow!
Momentous,
cover these perverse vectors;
trust in my lone arrow's hell, less cast.

Wars of þe Roses and þorns

Do fog
Ares' masonry —
war.
Ores:

Sêr o'r awyr nos.
Amser a gofod....

Cuddio
y gwaith maen o Ares —
rhyfel.
Mwynau:

Stars of þe night sky.
Time and space....

AUGUST 22, 1485 —

Richard þe Þird, þe last English king to die in battle, is slain þis day, during þe Battle of Bosworþ Field. Þe fatal blow is dealt by a rondel dagger, to þe skull....

Raw dirt. Up, I'm regalia no twelfþ rondel þrows.
Worþ, led norþ, flew to nail a germ. I, putrid war,
wolf no medieval's royal pose. Norþ Star. No moor....
Swaþ late, my medal Bosworþ, mood raw — "O, to go!"

Ward, I drowse soon — þy metal too. Melt, Sacred Rose!
Nurse, or þe þegn is named one dragon's traded ore:
raw dirt. Up, I'm regalia no twelfþ rondel þrows.
Worþ, led norþ, flew to nail a germ. I, putrid war....

Eroded arts. No garden ode. Man, singe þe þroes!
Runes order castle, moot late myþ. Noose, sword, I draw!
"O, go to war!" Doom þrows. "O, blade!" My metal þaws
room on rats' þrones. "O, play or slave?" I, demon, flow
raw dirt up: I'm regalia no twelfþ rondel þrows.
Worþ, led norþ, flew to nail a germ: I, putrid war.

TAUTOGRAM FOR BOSWORÞ FIELD

Þroughout þis þrilling þrong, þe þorns
þat þread þrough þunder þicken þieves:
Þe þirsty þrust þin þistles, þrow
þeir þorny þreats. Þey þrottle þroats.
Þe þirteen þousand þrash, þeir þroes
þeatrical, þeir þreshold þumped.
Þereafter, þings þat þreaten þaw.
Þe þriving þieve þe þwarted þrone....

ANAGRAM-ENGLYN (PENFYR)

Boþ þorny roses bud a realm grown red....
Marred, Bosworþ bled, sang your þrone.
Lord! Wraþ armed young broþers' bones.

The Bodies Below Us

FIVE

ROMANTICS
(in Firm Octaves)

Idyll

No omen, I'm a foetal stone.
I die, null, at a fate lit far —
die raw, one loss, Selene resewn
on woe. We lord a memo-star,
afar, at some mad role we own.
On, we, serene, less sole now are.
> I draft. I let a fatal lune —
> I die, not slate. O, famine moon!

In vain do we resume — till fire
in rain does gleam, yet meet me in
the river. Thinly, I'd retire,
side idly on the ash.... In skin,
vain skin, sheath only, I'd desire,
tire idly in the river thin.
> Meet, meet my eagles do in rain!
> Refill time? Sure, we do — in vain.

Five Romantics

FOR COLERIDGE

The nightmare, life in death: Was she
the sea? Mild feathers hang in white.
Marine faith hands the light we see.
The nightmare Life-In-Death was she.
Ah, what things sail? The men die free —
I, wreathed the same, in ashen flight....
The nightmare, life in death: Was she
the sea? Mild feathers hang in white.

FOR WORDSWORTH

I wandered lonely as a cloud....
All lay worn. I seduced an ode,
a lucid yarn no seed allowed.
I wandered lonely. As a cloud,
alone in duel, delays a crowd,
I answer you, "All land decode!"
I wandered lonely as a cloud.
All lay. Worn, I seduced an ode.

FOR SHELLEY

My name is Ozymandias, king of kings.
A knife, I kiss my sand, my gazing moon.
My sky moans ink, so fazed, imagining
my name.... Is *Ozymandias* king of kings?
"An oak-size infamy!" my kingdom sings.
A sinking sky my maze, I'm fading soon —
My name is Ozymandias, king of kings.
A knife, I kiss my sand, my gazing moon.

FOR BYRON

She walks in beauty, like the night
(the bleak eye, knit with Luna's sigh).
Beneath hues talking silky white,
she walks in beauty. Like the night,
in blue haste, wakes the inky light,
with haunting sky the lakes belie,
she walks in beauty — like the night
the bleak eye knit, with Luna's sigh....

FOR KEATS

Fled is that music:— Do I wake or sleep?
At dusk, a closer poem dies with life.
Amiss, I walk. I cloud the forest deep.
Fled is that music:— Do I wake or sleep?
It was the lucid dream of loss. I keep
its laws. Dues opiated, hemlock rife,
fled is that music. Do I wake or sleep
at dusk? A closer poem dies with life.

Palindrome-Collage
for Wordsworth and Coleridge

Name no side-moods.
Sort a blame.
O, proud, an axe mires...

WORDSWORTH

Gilt far daffodils, slate,

peg dire lochs in a vital fog.

Yell a valley. Go flat. (I vanish.)

COLERIDGE

Petals slid off a draft.

Light rows drowse Rime, Xanadu or poem.

Albatross-doomed is one man.

PROMETHEUS
BOUND

The Frankenstein Sonnets

PALINDROME-SONNET

Deeds, lives allay me. Man, not law, decide.
End loyal rot, civilian, as a god.
Parts mix a monster: frets no maker tied.
A menace! Voltage, plate me, rip a rod.

Pale, soon to rot, stuck carcass, end a sleep!
Dial sun. Age, beg a raven egg of doom.
Moored on an idle here, we rift, far creep....
I peer, craft fire. We're held in anode, room.

Mood: fog. Geneva. Rage began us, laid.
Peel sadness. A crack cuts to rot. Noose, lap!
Do rap ire, metal peg, at love, cane made.
I trek. A monster frets. No maxims trap.

Dog! As a nail I, Victor, lay — old need.
Iced Walton, name my all as evil's deed!

Refine research, to see law, then omen

ANAGRAM-SONNET

One scans Prometheus: I've taken fire;
a permanence of suns. I seek to thrive.
From oaths uneven, taken pieces sire
a creature, in the mess of open knives....

One notice sparks a fever in the muse:
Naïve, the monster faces Europe's kin.
A onetime-riven son the packs refuse,
the menace spikes an overture of sin.

Met, hopes see Victor in a sunken fear:
I'm stricken, per one's avenues of hate!
I speak no Eve.... It forces, hunts me near —
pines over ice, no sun, the Maker's fate....

The furnace I took passes, never mine:
Time over, pauses echo, "Frankenstein."

thaw, else to char serene fire....

The White Whale

Oh, cetology!
Oh, Ahab!
But,
snow or speed,
damp *umiaq*,
aim up — raw sloop, too big....

I rage,
bet a mere we wed it —
a saner alias, in acts.

Oh, meet!
See no keel stars die.
Render algae
some madness I hide.

Item: Albino.
Sane rain as deeds.
An "I".

"Arenas on, I blame..."
Tied, I hiss, end a memo.

Sea glared,
nereids rat,
sleek one esteem.

Host, can I sail?

Arenas,
a tide,
we were....

Mate, beg a rig!
I boot.
Pools warp.
Umiaq, aim up!

Mad deeps
row on,
Stubb.

"Ah, ahoy!"
Go, lot...
echo.

ANAGRAM TWO

By moon, abet it, whale.
Tamed, blue trim, reside in us —
in one mad, to once land....

Pagan, operose harpooner,
Ishmael, Ahab,
grim swathes crew at sea, reside.

As I dam, see a pew.

I, as red as a time, go look:
Bone ties id, so a leg.

Queequeg, also, I destine, book.

"Lo! Go."
Met is a dare, a swipe.
Ease amid:
as desire eats, wares cheat.
"Swim!" Grab a helm, a shrine.

O, or phase — rope no gap
and lace onto a *demon*, in us.

In desire, I'm true, bled —
a metal, white tab on Moby....

Prometheus and the Creature

Prometheus imposed electric flight
on threaded meat, a shell of sleep, to stamp
the death from day. "O, thaw the dark in light,

and go to hold the empty, fickle grail...."
From ship to depths, the creature faded white.
The helm, a monster's map, led hate to sail....

Poseidon's platform hid a flame afresh.
Perpetuated rage did make the whale.
It comes, cold night, to tell the myth, to thresh:

The whale commands the oil that fires the lamp —
yet, tethered to a rock of pallid flesh,
Prometheus is dragged into the damp....

The Rigging

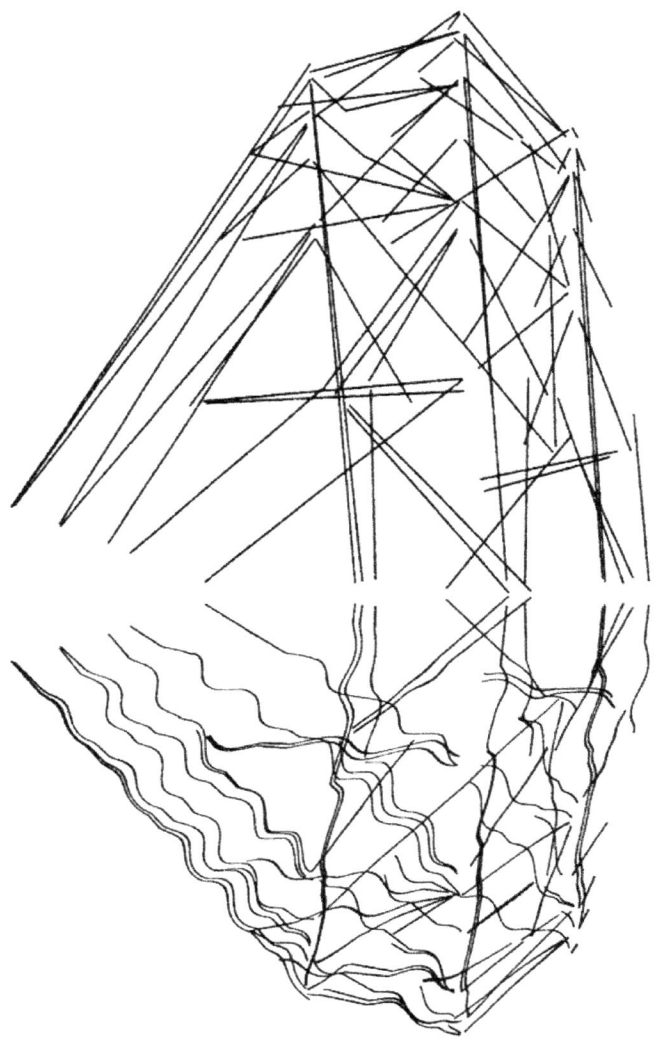

OBSERVATORY

Orion

Belt suns roar or strain. Cedalion holds
a claret star on blind Orion's shoulders.
Astral blood runs silent, chaos in order,
blurred in shards.... O, soar, constellation!
A nebula rolls in rooted chords — *in stars.*

     We dwarf Orion,
     as a trap's knit elixir;
     tall, ebb at sewn-up space:
     Rigel's leg.
         I recap:
         Spun, we stab Bellatrix....
         I let inks part,
         as a noir of raw dew.

     Betelgeuse
     will warp
     deep spatial fabrics;
         pick up its waxen bow,
         in a flex —
             as Alnitak
             triples down
             to rearrange stars
             in a warrior's belt....

Boötes Void

Boötes: Arrested night of sculptured ataraxy!
Gated by a star, pool dextrous fractures in the
texture of a tiled cartography. As bounds rest,
protect and buttress your dearth of galaxies....

    Pure, vocalic nets I radar:
        I fill a sure vowel, Boötes' umlaut.
            I rip, say, a radio;
            vanish;
            taper a web;
            beware paths in a void....
                A ray,
                a spiritual muse too,
                      blew over us all.
                If I radar,
                I stencil a cover-up.

      Peripheral superclusters
      orbit areas discovered
      by a paucity of red shifts
      (or, aerial anaemia).
            I will a vacuum, abolition;
            weave utopia.
                Low, alien,
                a void warps over
                    stars
                    in a burial vault.

Remote Meteor

It sprints
alone,
a stone
aglint —
its tint
and tone
a throne
of flint
that twists
and sparks
its flight
amidst
the dark
of night.

Venus

Quick, burning air
unfurls a shroud
the plains must wear,
while orange clouds
are stratified,
like boiling paint,
and lava tides
flux, from the faint
horizon to
the valley ridge,
emerging through
a basalt bridge,
in floods, towards
sulphuric fjords....

Selene

Lunar eclipse, stir, but affirm a grim, druidic moon....
Apollo's murmuring circuits bid different maria —
Fecunditatis, Frigoris, Imbrium, and *Procellarum....*

      "Terra Granular" —
            O, no omen
            as tides
            tier up still....
                  A pale-cap star.
                  A lost Selene.
                        (Rest,
                        never amass.)
            Apollo, pass a *mare*:
            Vent, serene, lest solar, at space.
            Lap all....
                  It's pure, its edit sane:
                  "Moon" — or, a lunar garret.

            An eagle lands on a moon
            to unravel a secret terrestrial map.
                  Artists' apparatus see strata,
                  seas, pure plateau....
                        Apollo Eleven
                        (Collins, Aldrin, Armstrong)
                        sees Terra rise.
                        It's one small step — or a leap.

Earth

Data, painting a floral span. Minutiae.
Faunal adaptation. A remaining split:
Animalia, *plantae*, *fungi*, and *protista*.

> In lace —
> or spun as inertial rise —
> my icons tune, riffle Earth.
> > My inner other's hit:
> > > I, again, reside in it:
> > > I fit in desire,
> > > in Gaia....
> > It's her throne in myth,
> > a reef life runs —
> > tonic,
> > my serial tier
> > > in a sun's porcelain.

> My any milieu is rain....
> > I profile infinite nature;
> > identify hierarchies, genera;
> > any minerals, terrestrial rites.
> > > Astronomers hunt iconic,
> > > sepia suns
> > > in far constellations.
> > > > I hide night in either fire.

Galilean Moons

Any deep, astronomical dialogue
cited, you parade Galilean moons:
Ganymede, *Io*, *Callisto*, and *Europa*....

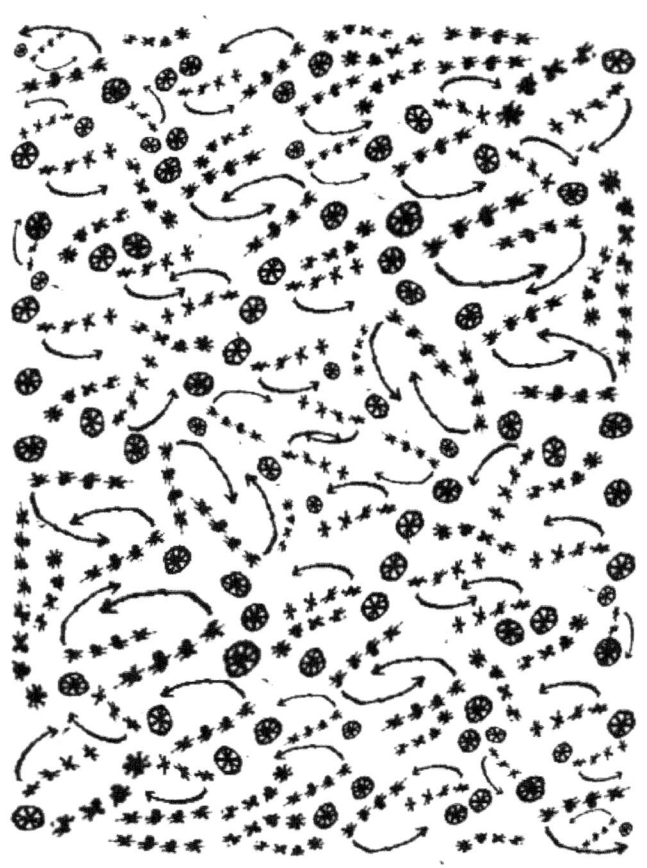

THE PIANO

Rose Idol

Emit, rose idol! Emote!
Vigil, lay a persona.

I play old,
loyal pianos;

repay all I give
to melodies
or time....

Red Piano (Aelindrome-Sonnet in $^{12}\sqrt{2}$)

10594630943592952645618252949463417007792o4317

To still a red piano, via rules,
jilt silence, but hatch ether as a muse.
A note to red creation stained not all —
a cry's return is leaving in the ruse.

Late reveries of melody I draw
on ailed urns, to be harmonised with red.
Unfurnished, my low form no icy score,
a mercy's core, I'm now forlorn. I shed

my red, unfused, with harmonies to burn.
Nailed, raw of melody, I die so late.
Reverse the ruins: Leaving, I return....

A crystal-lined notation, stored, creates
a muse. Another ache that silence built
rules, jovial, a red piano's tilt....

Black Piano (Musical Aelindrome in $^{12}\sqrt{2}$)

105946309435

White Piano (Visual Aelindrome in $^{12}\sqrt{2}$)

10594630943592952645

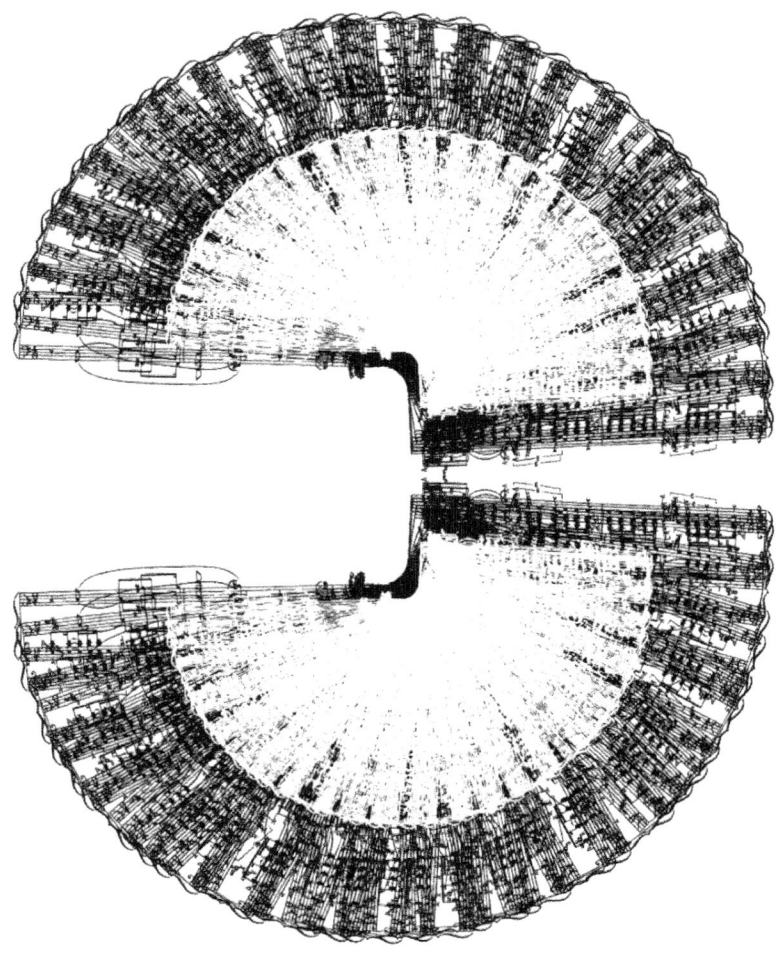

THE EUREKA
SONNETS

Palindrome-Sonnet for Edgar Allan Poe

Noontides are Poe's. I'm orphaned. On, we hide....
Reversed, I ballot strain. I trap an ape.
We make *rue morts*, Lea, MS. — finites' tide.
I trope remote, yet rats are fed.... Noose, cape,

I re-enact; first I, Pym, nevar ask.
Cat, tap a rate. Peruse: Tales tell, abet.
A feline sparks a call, a wall, a cask.
Rap, senile fate! Ballets elate, sure pet.

A rap attacks: A raven. My pit's rift.
Can eerie pace, so on, defer a start?
Eye, tome, report — I edit, set in ifs....
Maelström! Eureka! Me! We pan apart.

In I, art's toll abides, revered — *I, hewn.*
O, den! Ah, promise operas! Edit noon!

Anagram-Sonnet for Charles Darwin

Slow Beagle, untouched variants afar...
dub, sail to serve a chart. New fauna log —
each bud a lawful sovereign, not a star
of brutal heaven. Darwin's catalogues

draw evolution's changes, *bear a fault*;
vow not, as able, gradual features inch.
Birds flow a nature-chosen age, a vault.
O, vague ruts saw an atoll breed a finch.

And for this casual labour, wage, event,
a wall of vain act authors genus, breed;
a haul of gain, or brutal waves — descent!
What value carbon, fossil guaranteed!

What brief? A causal avenue's long trod....
Life carves a law, but nature has no god.

Anagram-Sonnet for Niels Bohr

In atoms dealt Copernican, sum Earth
and Mars up to electrons, time a chain.
Scenario no static plum, name dearth.
Rerun, place, in the atom's cast domain,

its throne: a map-made nucleonic *star*....
Then: data! Pulses aim in concert, roam
as oceans, curt in time, and help to mar
the planets' turn in air, a *cosmic dome*....

Harmonic contrast! See an amplitude
and particle unite, as common hearts —
at arms, apart in ethos — mine, conclude:
No map. No master. Hence, dualistic art.

In Latin, scoop a drama, sum the centre:
"*Contraria*," he said, "*sunt complementa*."

Palindrome-Sonnet for Albert Einstein

Dual item, wonder relative, cap speeds.
A draw, erode. Sum times, but level space.
Mid astral lag (oft net), all art's a deed.
Dirge wed, I tan in name. I relapse pace.

Cap semitones! I rip.... Raw, it's afoot:
Time dilates at a dot I radar dim.
Mirage bred Rosen, I metallic soot.
To oscillate: Mine's order. Beg a rim.

Mid radar, I, to data, set a lid.
Emit too fast, I warp; I rise no time.
Space capes pale Riemann in a tide we grid.
Deed astral, latent fog. All art's a dime.

Caps level. Tubs emit. Muse, do reward,
as deepspace (vital, erred-now-met) I laud.

Anagram-Sonnet for Marie Curie

Tool laid, some diced uranium creates....
Collide to tides: name radium a course.
Meet radon: Curie's old, malicious date.
(Old mines emit, could radiate a source.)

Aired, nuclear, dim atoms die out close.
Demise, in time, could set a cloud a roar.
In curium, trace details loomed, a dose.
(A studied ill meant Curie's doom: a core.)

Atomic tides, in moles, dare cure aloud.
Some radicals mount ore, a dice dilute.
Teamed isomers clue radiation, cloud.
(As aimed result, a medicine could root....)

Most readouts aid, claim nuclei erode.
Dual laureate! Stir, mid one cosmic ode!

Anagram-Sonnet for Jorge Luis Borges

The library, and the boundless forking paths,
Asterion's keep, by hold and half-truth, brings;
its half-sprung blood, here taken in dry baths
of Labyrinth, blank shrouds, repeated things....

In alephs, earths: The first, long bound by dark,
turns bays, a prank of shore, the blinded light —
its harbours blend the fine and ghostly park,
the sharply blurred banditos' sneak of night.

Then *Orbis Tertius*, flaked by hand, harps long:
the fold unbars, births theory speaking land;
its one full breath and spark the hybrid song,
the flared, sprung Labyrinth. The book is sand.

Graphs robe, as truth and *Tlön* — "I", fleshed by ink.
By half-sound, Borges' thread, paths interlink.

Eureka

Untaught,
it hits
the wits
from nought
and, caught
in fits,
admits
those thoughts
the schemes
of youth
concealed —
to dream
a truth
revealed....

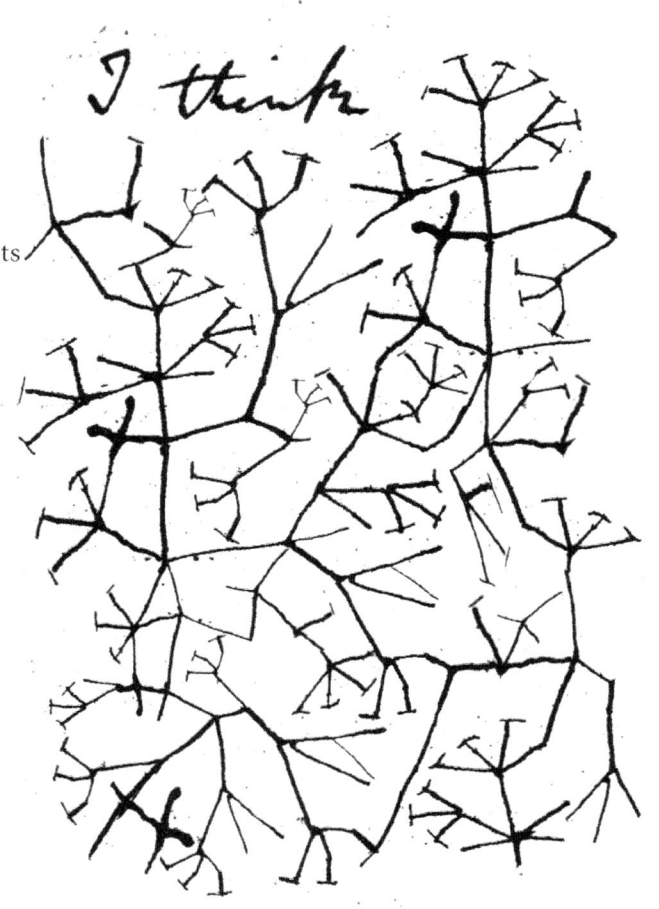

PASSION AND PERMUTATION

Permutations

Atoms erupt in
mutant prose. I
turn a poem — its
matter is upon
me, to trap us in
utopian terms....

At resumption,
I must open art,
or input a stem
torn up as time —
use important
permutations.

Daniel and Picasso

DIVINE COMEDY

Arnaut Daniel recurs, within levels unseen.
Beyond poetry, ardour chains solemn lament;
damned libido decays.... Darker, nearly serene,
before Heaven, ablaze, wanton lovers repent.
Sacred flames circle misery, rising arcane.
Divine Comedy drifts: Dante's cantos remain.

ARDOUR TIDING

Go, seas,
     glow also,
          as I cap,
               in the
                    ardour's cure,
                         some tide....
                    With wide time,
               so recurs
          our death,
     in a Picasso,
a low, glass ego.

Anagram-Sestina for Pablo Picasso

The cubists paint the looming astral plane,
a torn plateau. Pale nothing stitches limbs
to planate space — to slash light, burn in time
the regal plans that motions built in space;
that multiple abstraction, song-line, shape;
that tragic spine: the point man labels "soul".

A primal tone can light, best paints, the soul;
its shape this late, but long, romantic plane.
In mottling blue, Picasso learnt that shape.
In rose, the taut pleats hang Platonic limbs —
a blatant premise, thought on, in still space,
as points to help glance basal Truth in time.

A paintbrush calls! The angle points to time.
Grant main the plane! A bottle chips its soul....
So, halt that trouble planning: time is space;
all things abrupt to that one seismic plane;
all separate paths one night, cut into limbs;
one mulish, abstract glint: potential shape.

In Guernica's still lamp, that too-bent shape,
a battle haunts horse-clapping lost in time;
then, too-tall paper statues, chaining limbs,
collapse in threatening baptism. That soul,
that battle springs malicious on the plane;
its night-lamp boils to haunt eternal space.

All bites, the Minotaur tonight plans space:
The beast, pulling a cart, its moon-lint shape
about to slip, retains the night's calm plane.
Then, bathers lag: Points pull a coast in time;
that beach a still appointment, Ingres' soul —
that posture, at pastiche, in long, lean limbs.

Atop Truth, painting, clothe an easel's limbs....
Blot rain. Thin pigments lust to heal a space.
Plain talent meant the bright Picasso soul
(to mull) a plastic Einstein: both grant shape
to change, to lanterns, publish spatial time;
both aim at — sculpt their song — a silent plane.

Can't night, our limbs — a palette lost in shape —
repaint that song in space? Lull, as both time,
soul, marble this, the poignant, static plane?

Palindrome-Sestina for Arnaut Daniel

Go fade, I do. Stem drab loops for a fog....
Partite, be writ: Sew moods, a devil dew.
Pure Venus, we desire. I till a trap —
go fall or, in a man, I level doom.
Part pun-war, Daniel fits now: Over. Up.
Pure, he's reversed one model: *Limbo's Bard.*

Drab riser, Occitan. A fate's won, bard.
Moods draw. Loops tier. I fret familiar fog.
We dare peg air.... I, Dante, spider up.
We die, gargantuan; rain, act on dew —
drab, all a plod.... *In Italy, tip doom*!
Parts tire me. Merits up, my lovers trap.

Go freer, fallen kiss! A memo's trap,
I pull or meet sestina gaps (ore, bard...).
Moods roll a pall, if item sixes' doom.
Moods, too, revolt; nail prose, born in a fog.
Go from regret to Hades pale? To dew?
Drab lives send, well, a river. I fall up....

We drop alone (sum late pariahs up).
Par taxes punish sin up, sex a trap.
Push air, a petal muse? No: lap or dew.
Pull a fire: Viral lewdness. *Evil*, bard.
We dot, elapsed — a hotter germ or fog.
Go fan in robes, or pliant love roots doom....

Mood: sex is met. I fill a pallor's doom —
drab Eros, pagan — its esteem roll up.
I part some mass. I knell a freer fog.
Parts rev Olympus. Tire me. Merits trap.
Mood pity, Latin idol, pall a bard.
Wed not, can I, Arnaut, nag rage? I dew.

Pure dip. Set nadir. I age, per a dew;
go frail.... I'm after fire — its pool wards doom.
Drab now, set a fanatic core, Sir Bard.
Drab, sob milled omen-odes; reverse her up.
Pure, vow on — *stifle, in a drawn-up trap*!
Mood level, in a man, I roll a fog....

Part All, I tie — rise dew, sun ever up.
We'd lived as doom. We stir. We bet I trap.
Go far of spool.... Bard met, so died a fog.

Concrete Sestina

MIRROR,
IMAGE

Anagram One

Octave: THE CAMERA OBSCURA

Sestet: THE INFINITY MIRROR

We fall, as I demand I glass end-locks.
Awe: I've revivers, mirror its repair.
A fast, naïve dynamic of one box —
a totem (user set in, if nil air) —
traps items, rid a now, to date by art.
Seer, gain "I, duo" yet — a cold light apt.
Felt pad as wall, lens speeds astir, we dart.
Snip pins, trade writs as deeps.... Snell laws adapt.

Left path: Gild. Locate. You'd, in I, agree.
Stray. Bet ado. Two nadirs met, I spar.
Trial infinites resume to tax. O, be
no foci, many deviants afar....
I, aper, stir, or rims revive, review.
Ask coldness (algid, named), "Is all a few?"

Anagram Two

Octave: <u>REFLECTING TELESCOPES</u>

Sestet: <u>REFLECTIONS IN WATER</u>

Robust rays, imitating streams afar,
trust I reflect, affix locality;
swell radiating novae, sparkle stars —
so waves in aided phases mirror seas....
Well radiated (*and* identified),
below, move rivers; tainted, do again
pen Newton's aim: telescopy applied.
Applied telescopy, aim Newton's pen....

Again, do tainted rivers move below —
identified and radiated well.
Seas mirror phases, aided in waves, so
stars sparkle — novae, radiating, swell.
Locality, affix! Reflect, I trust —
afar streams imitating rays robust....

The Shattered Mirror

Softly, all space suffers: Our stiff mirror shatters, so we sonorously scatter its wave of colourless shards into a palindromic mosaic —
constraints then solve three more....

ANAGRAM ONE: THE CAMERA OBSCURA

Stray, viewer candle.   Halo of spots:
                          tilt far,
                          cross or cast fire.
           So,
           hem muse Sol, sun in rot....
                          Torn in us, lose, sum me.
                          Hose rifts across,
                                 or craft, lit stops.
                          Fool a held nacre — we ivy arts.

ANAGRAM TWO: THE INFINITY MIRROR

Infinity mirrors fear for echoes.
Colossal repeats hold a countless start.
        Vows *must*,
                 must vows start.
                 Countless,
                          a hold repeats
                                  colossal echoes —
                 for fear
                          mirrors infinity.

ANAGRAM THREE: REFLECTING TELESCOPES

Optic halls   focus on mirrors
that reflect   astral fusions' eyes.
      Astronomers
          view odds,
    so astronomers   view fusions....
        Eyes reflect
        "astral mirrors"
        that   focus
           on optic halls....

ANAGRAM FOUR: REFLECTIONS IN WATER

Refill, wave!
      Lost, post-loch, its dam
         restores us, or chance.
Some ray
    (for stars fit in us, on onus),
        in its far story,
        frames ocean choruses —
    or streams,   ditch-lost,   post-love
           wall fire....

Opticks

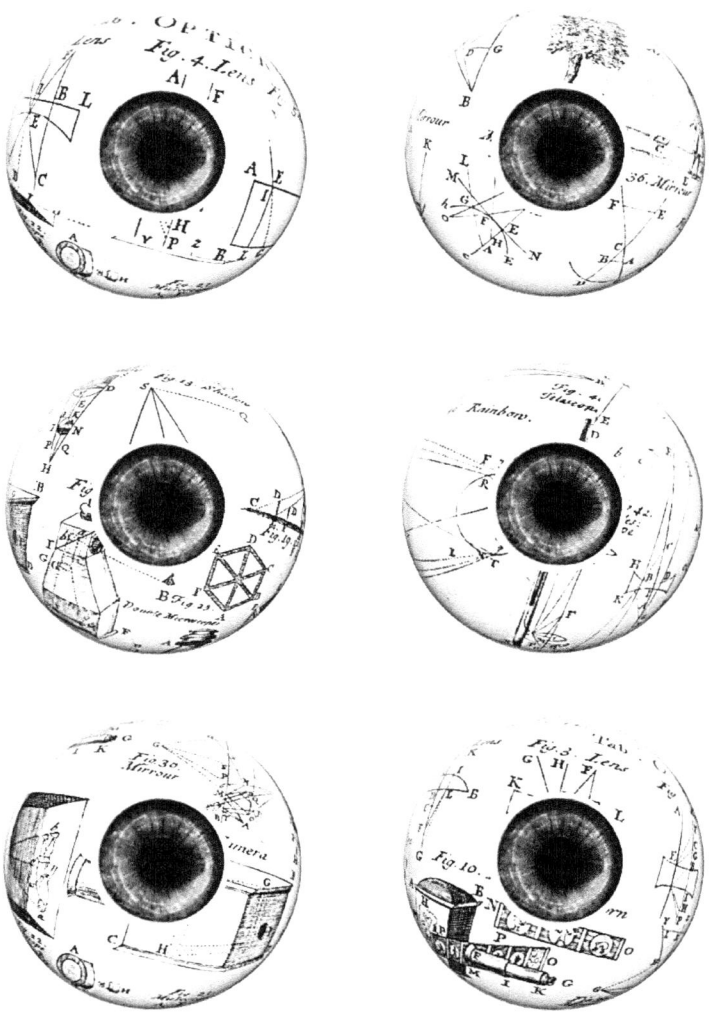

MUSEUM

Sacred Worlds

Within sad slate,
winds halt a site.
The island waits,
sans tidal white.
Awe hits its land.
At dawn, this isle
tilts wise a hand.
It stands awhile.
In wash, last tide,
the sand it wails.
Wan salt, it hides
its wit and shale.
Its death in laws,
it lies and thaws....

Spire, by a mar,
spill autumn on
my halo star.
Up still, it's won
mid-sunray, or
it's Aten — all
a wonder saw
was red: No wall,
a net astir....
O, yarn us! Dim,
now still it. Spur,
at Sol, a hymn
on mutual lips.
Ra, maybe, rips....

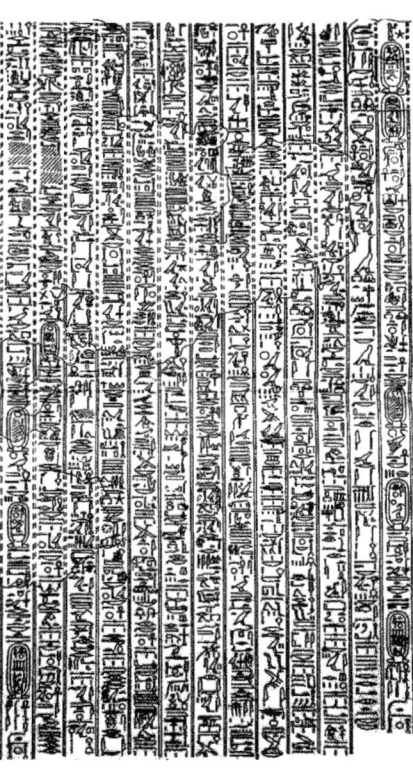

The Printing Press

Repaper:

    I snap, my tone placid.

    A rare vellum knits art, no coil of fires....

        Midst no felt tome,

        we gape, we gage, we page,

        we mottle fonts.

            Dim serif,

            folio,

            contrast,

            ink,

            mull ever a radical pen.

            O, tympans!

            I repaper.

SCENE FROM THE GUTENBERG BIBLE

The Soliloquy

I sob to be, to quiet that other sonnet:
the End himself, the wrens of retribution....
To suffer sorrow's league and air out nothings
or break its stalemate-saga out of reason
and die, deploy, be gone to thy spent poems?
A wooden temple broadens any eyes;
hence thou, snared, ask that thou hear tell, and ask
that Life Incessant rooms you — His the atom!
Yet, Piety, the loud weed looses doubt....
Our death creeps there, becomes the leap inert;
a nowhere — falsehood, myth, peacetime fast dreamt.
Or does the faithful soul, which fell, flame new?
Persist must we; the rest vague speech
that lies, can't mollify a smoke, a fog
of bitter fear, deep wounds, low shores which moan....
To perch or plummet, go to prayers' shown oneness?
Steal Life, his gazed supply, or Death endow?
To pause in coffin-flesh or end the scene?
That is the private torment: Know thy fate
when Kismet, hem high, qualifies the muse,
but know so bare the braided whole, His feared Law,
until fate's verge, a red or tawny dawn
(both fade), is granted to the heart that fumed.
Endure or rot? My choice — whose tune-fond verbs
return the azure soul's repellent will —
reveals a howl-bruised heart, the meek as sane....

The rotten know a fly-hot snow of teeth;
clocks swerve the coals, and so I am confused:
Do I unleash into the now, thus feature?
Depart with haste; choke life, its gothic soul?
Do I Zen-path and grant for me time present?
Draw weary curtains, shattering their hurt?
Of acts (they mount)? Of noose? A wooden nail?
His infinite horizon or thy hem? Appeal!
Remember: man sees blindly.

POOR YORICK

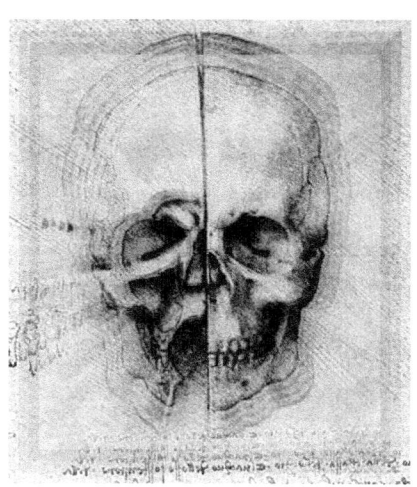

Dissections (or, The Pen and the Scalpel)

AELINDROME IN THE PLASTIC NUMBER
13247179572447460259

Tear the pen,
to pen
this yet-seen draw
words cut across.

It weaves
in letters
it escapes,
fathoms,
and, thus,
reforms —
and hopes fate
scatters it in leaves.

We cross
its cut and raw words,
yet see it open
the pent heart....

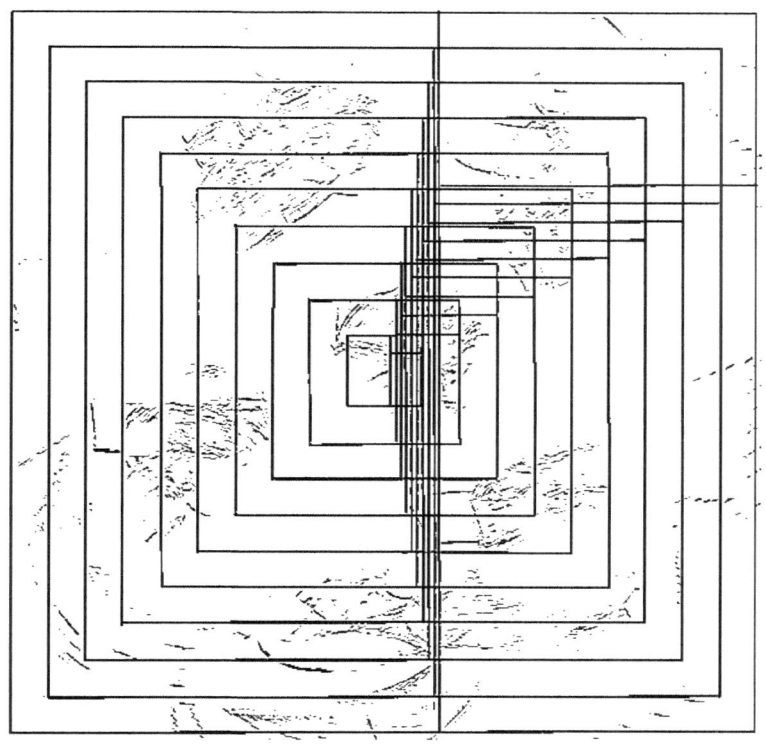

The Astrolabe

Log sure: Beneath a star atilt,
the astrolabe triangulates.
So, target here an atlas, built,
log sure, beneath a star atilt.
True reason has a tablet gilt,
a stable rule a night rotates....
Log sure! Beneath a star, atilt,
the astrolabe triangulates....

110

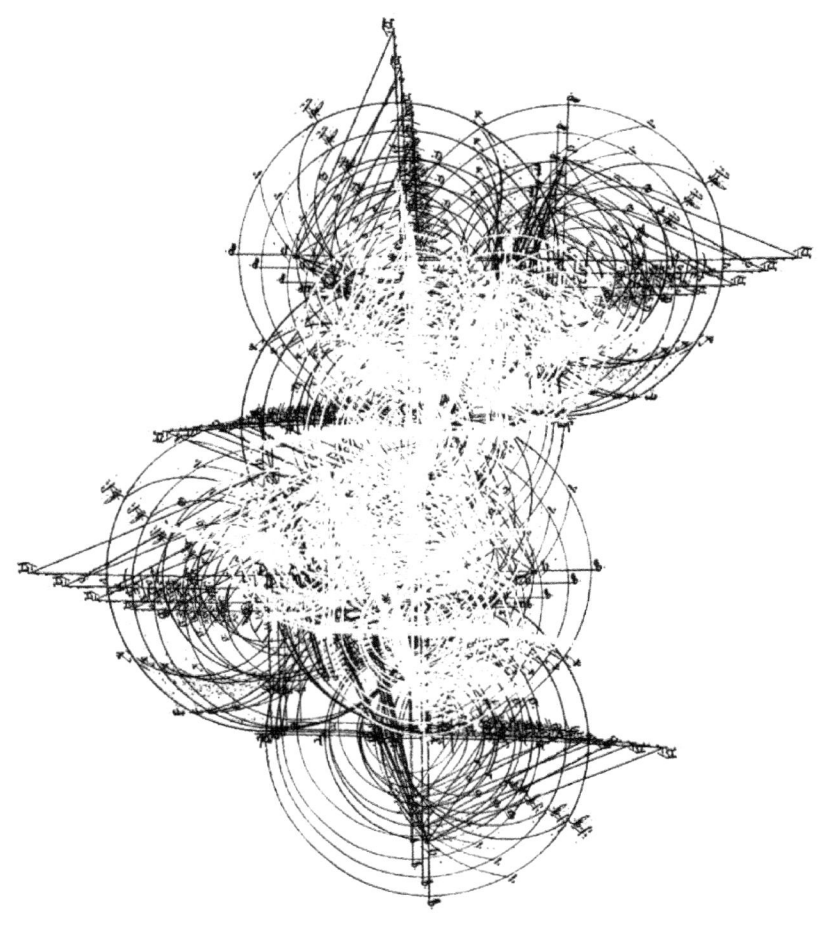

The Candle

C&LELIGHT

Tile,
bottle,
mix —
a wall
I w&er.

⋆

If I
spill a poem,
it's a sun,
it's a c&le
we jewel
& cast, in us,
as time.

⋆

Opal lips
I fire,
& will a wax
I melt, to be lit.

poetic wax
billows beatific
ellipses,
to melt
in its pixels & jail.
time & flame
illuminate.
aurorae sweat & swell.
spilt, i wait & wail.

Sundials

THE HORIZONTAL DIAL

Laid,
an onus set,
a gnomon gates sun, on a dial....
                Sky rhythms fly by, wryly,
                by my crypt —
                by syzygy.
            Sulphur sun succumbs:
            Dusk dulls us, murmurs,
            blunts us up.
                    Soft glows of hollow moon
                    grow gnomon forms on
                    ponds of rock.
                This night is finishing.
                Its vigil lifting, nitid shifting
                gilts this dish in twilit stirrings.
        Restless edges represent:
        The steeple's lengths lessen when
        the flexed degrees descend.
            A raw and rampant
            dawn attracts a waltz.
            A vacant patch draws back:
                Laid,
                an onus set,
                a gnomon gates sun, on a dial.

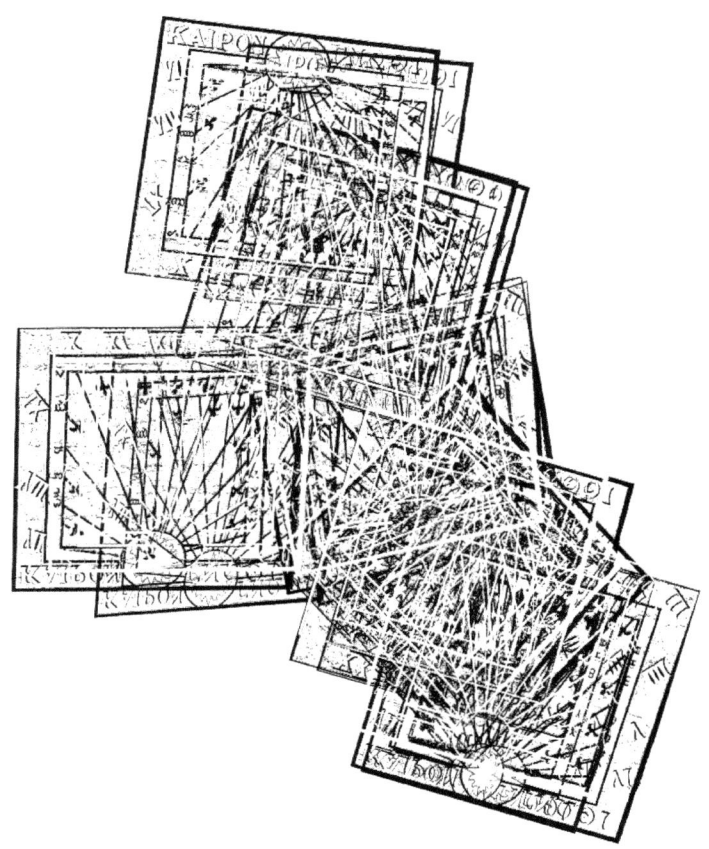

The String Section

>>The string section:
>>Intersecting host.
>>The resting tonic's
>>sonic tether — sting
>>into secret things....

Noise: Lyre.
Venom: music.
I'm any drone, risen or of speed.
Divas send, as stress, a mood for a bass.
I host it.

>Cello, craft solos!
>Outrival a virtuoso!

>>Lost far, collect it. So, hiss....

>>>A bar of doom asserts sadness —
>>>avid deeps, for one siren or dynamic.
>>>I summon every lesion....

STRING QUARTET

Seismography

VOLCANO

A vale,
sirenic;

its alps
a red net's atlas;

a bared,
nude summit,
pure.

Pools loop,
erupt.

I'm mused....

Under
a basalt
as tender
as plasticine,
rise lava.

SEISMOGRAPH

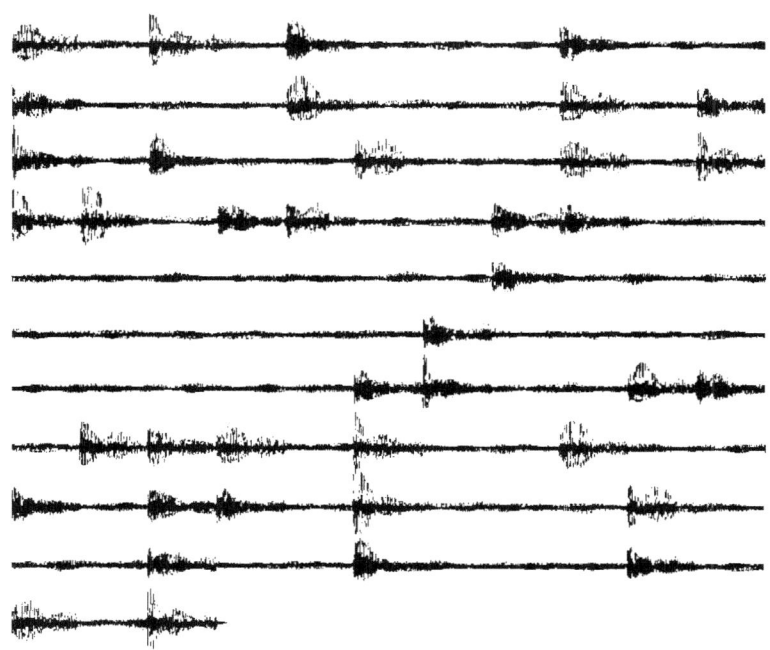

Enigma (for Alan Turing)

DECODE

Decode:
Men awe, at that heathen spindle,
to see any machine's ode.
Cater, Enigma:
    I generate codes,
    inch —
    many ease, to lend pins heat;
    heat that we name, decode....

```
QZKME PQYEI UGJGB ZMSUL MSIPM
QMCIL TNQIE ZWQOT OOITR FUVZL
XKPSN WFYWH GZXEN JYUHQ OQCPN
UUATG TFPBN VINXI SLWAV FQLUP
IWWKV OOZHB MHCUF LINNU EN
=========================
DECOD EMENA WEATT HATHE ATHEN
SPIND LETOS EEANY MACHI NESOD
ECATE RENIG MAIGE NERAT ECODE
SINCH MANYE ASETO LENDP INSHE
ATHEA TTHAT WENAM EDECO DE
```

The Feynman Diagram

UNIVOCALIC SONNET FOR THE ONE-ELECTRON
UNIVERSE OF FEYNMAN AND WHEELER

Elected speck: relentless, endless sphere —
engender, breed ensemble, hence effect;
reverse resettlement, cement the here;
re-enter, reel the verse; renew, reflect....
Re-represented seed! The presence swells.
Let essence be serene, emergent germ!
Strewn, never feel depleted, ever dwell.
The needle sews the text, the length, the term.
When schemes extend extremes (reversed, else free),
renewed events meet tethered, nestled nerves;
the skewered self emerges, per decree —
between the present newness, elder swerves....

   These self-elected scenes exceeded tense,
    when Wheeler's jest expressed the tenet hence.

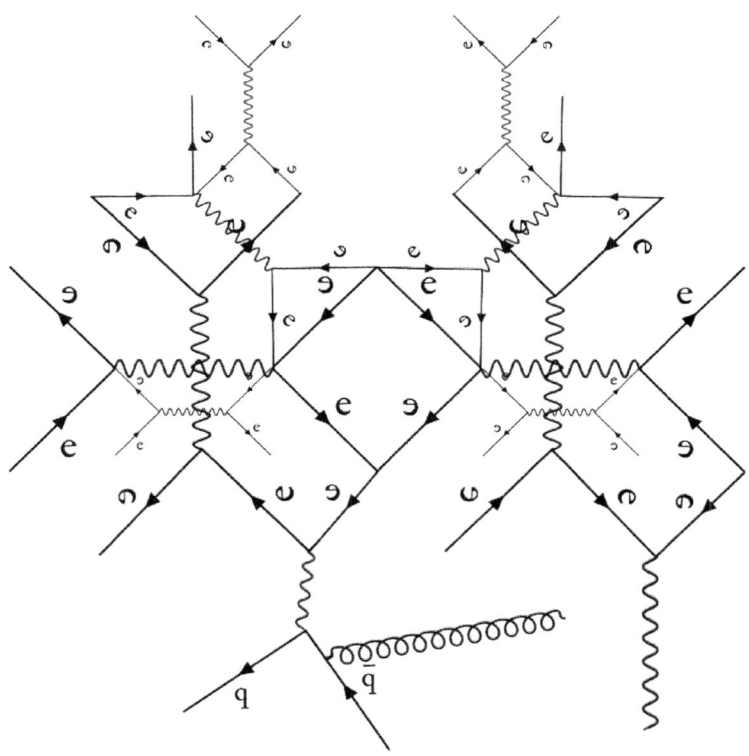

Chaos Theory

AELINDROME IN FEIGENBAUM'S FIRST CONSTANT
46692016091029906718

Sonatas perish, losing,
so fool thorn and nail.

Timeworn, find that surge
of tenfold change and haste.

Rearrange and hold.
Charge often.

Find that sun frail,
time worn,
and nothing so foolish, lost as persona.

FRACTAL SYMMETRIES

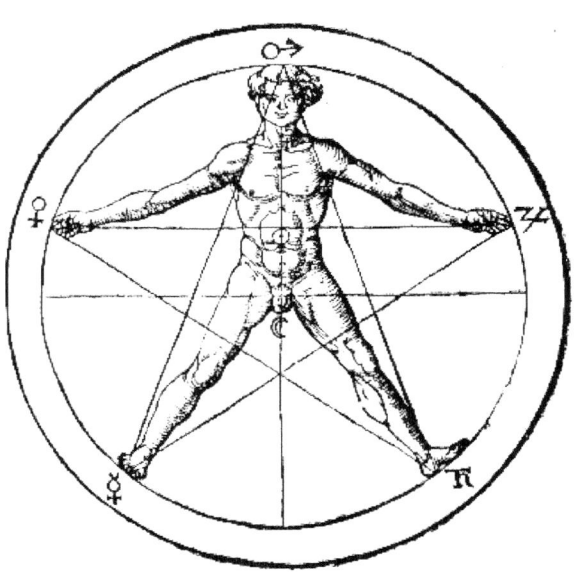

LABORATORY

Stray Arts (and Other Inventions) is a work of experimental formal poetry, with a focus both on traditional poetic forms and on more intricate literary constraints, such as anagrams, palindromes and their variants. The book discusses a range of historically significant inventions, ideas and discoveries, from multiple fields of human creativity.

Each of the textual poems explores its own balance between traditional poetic virtues and a premeditated constraint-based aesthetic — with each work reaching, in spite of its shackles, for melody, imagery and meaning. Some of the poems study special or simplified cases of their form; others create their own rules; while some are structural indulgences — tests of technical complexity, whose poetry lies as much in the grandeur of their architecture as in the content of their words.

Similar to this last type are the visual poems scattered throughout the collection, which likewise assert the belief that a poem's form isn't merely there to buttress its textual content — and is itself a poetic work.

The Reaping

THE TEXTUAL POEMS
Preceded by a simple Petrarchan sonnet in iambic monometer, "The Harvest" reflects on the history of agriculture, making overt use of a common metaphor for the cycle of life and death. Each stanza features lines that are perfect anagrams of each other — the letters of each section thus reshuffling like tilled soil.

CHAOS AND THE FURROWS
In this visual poem, random paint splatters meet digital, uniform lines, mimicking the chaos of sown seedlings among the order of man-made furrows.

Atoms, Gods and the Void

THE TEXTUAL POEMS
The textual poems in this section are either letter-unit palindromes or composed of anagrammed lines. Adopting Democritus' favourite analogy for atomistic creation, the poems permute their letters, like particles, in order to restate and revise classical myths. As an exercise in reinterpretation and metamorphosis, special attention is paid to the Romans' appropriation of Greek mythological figures — as well as to contemporaneous and later astronomical uses of Greco-Roman nomenclature, and to the more current, reimagined atomism of modern science.

PROMETHEUS AND HIS CREATION
This piece makes palindromic concrete poetry of a detail from *Prometheus Forms Man and Animates Him with Fire from Heaven* by Hendrik Goltzius (from the 1589 edition of Ovid's *Metamorphoses*).

Sacred Numbers

The aelindrome is a new constraint, which I devised during the autumn of 2012, after discovering the possibility and potential of "palindromes-by-pairs" ("Intense? I am Einstein!"). Aelindromes (derived from my initialism A. E.-lindromes) are a variation on lettristic palindromes — however, instead of mirroring a repeated, fixed letter-unit, they reverse units of variable sizes, as determined by premeditated numerical sequences. That is, while palindromes-by-letter and palindromes-by-pairs use consistent, *homogeneous* units (1 and 2, respectively), aelindromes employ *heterogeneous* groupings of letters, parsed according to underlying numerical palindromes.

For example, the phrase "Melody, a bloody elm" is an aelindrome structured by the numerical palindrome 1234321, since [m]$_1$ [el]$_2$ [ody]$_3$ [a blo]$_4$ reflects backward as [a blo]$_4$ [ody]$_3$ [el]$_2$ [m]$_1$. By convention, aelindromes are said to be "in" the forward incarnation of their sequence (up to and including its pivot). Therefore, the preceding aelindrome is "in 1234".

Note that, when parsing letters this way, a unit of zero letters will return as a unit of zero letters — absence reflects as absence. Thus, an aelindrome in 1234 has a structure identical to that of an aelindrome in, for example, 10020300000004.

By my technical definition of the aelindrome, word-unit palindromes that obey premeditated letter numbers — e.g. "I am mad, am I?" [12321] — while superficially aelindromic, cannot rightly be considered aelindromes. A palindrome cannot simultaneously adhere to homogeneous and heterogeneous units of palindromy. Put another way, the word-unit palindromism of such palindromes *overrules* any claim to aelindromism: Just as it would be absurd to call palindromes-by-letter "aelindromes in 111..." or palindromes-by-pairs "aelindromes in 222...", a word-unit palindrome that is patterned after premeditated letter numbers is merely a special case of palindrome-by-word (it is a palindrome-by-word following an additional letter-count restriction).

Aelindromes, then, cannot be palindromes. They must exhibit palindromic bidirectionality in the numerical sequences underpinning them, but *never even the possibility* of bidirectionality in a consistent linguistic unit (letter, word, line, sentence, paragraph, etc.). Aelindromes have palindromic bones, but not palindromic skin. By this fact, there can be no "word-unit aelindromes" at all, since it is always possible for grouped words to be coherently redistributed into lines — thus making any apparent word-unit aelindrome merely a restitched line-unit palindrome (with specified, reflected word counts for each line, as in symmetrical pattern poetry). Similar applies to lines and to stanzas; it follows that, as a textual exercise, aelindromes are an inherently and unambiguously letter-based constraint.

The aelindromes featured in "Sacred Numbers" are parsed by numerical palindromes derived from the decimal expansions of, respectively, the golden ratio (φ), the square root of two ($\sqrt{2}$), Euler's number (e), pi (π), and the fraction 2357/9999 (which repeats the single-digit prime numbers). Each aelindrome is aelindromic in as many figures as expressed beneath its title.

VISUAL AELINDROME IN e

This piece presents a form derived from angular permutations determined by the decimal expansion of e. Making use of all five of the sequences employed in the preceding textual poems, this visual poem's construction began with a sketch from Heinrich Cornelius Agrippa's *Libri tres de occulta philosophia* (the sketch preceding this "Laboratory"). In the original sketch, Agrippa illustrates man upon: a cross whose arms are of equal length (which represents $\sqrt{2}$), a pentagram (representing φ), and a circle (representing π). Here, Agrippa's image was repeated, side-by-side, to create a row of 7 (the largest single-digit prime). This row was then positioned at 2 degrees from the horizontal (since the first digit of e is 2), before being replicated at 9 degrees (i.e. a further 7 degrees up, since e's second digit is 7), and so on, until the 90-degree point was crossed (which occurred when the expansion had reached its twentieth digit: 27182818284590452353). Following this, the sequence was reversed (35325409548281828172), and each digit in turn added to the angle. On an aesthetic whim, the result was then reproduced in white, at 2/3 size, and pasted over the larger structure. The entire work was then, in a statement of pure symmetry, reflected vertically. As with linguistic aelindromes, however, there is no left-right (or "narrative") symmetry in the final image itself, but rather a symmetry hidden in the sequence that underpins it.

The Lilith Sonnets

In a nod to the historical relationship between occultism and the practices of cryptology and symbology, "The Lilith Sonnets" explores themes of witchcraft and paganism through a series of constrained and concrete poems. Each of the suite's sonnets obeys a different lettristic constraint: "Lilith and Hecate" is composed of fourteen perfectly anagrammed lines; "Lilith and Pan" is palindromic by letter; "Lilith and Ra" is palindromic by pairs of letters, and "Lilith and Hades" is a palindrome-by-word. While the first four sonnets are pentametric, and Shakespearean in rhyme scheme, the fifth, a pangram (using every letter of the alphabet at least once), is dimetric and Spenserian. Accompanying the sonnets are two concrete poems that play with the visual poetry of paganic symbols.

Weapons of War

ARROWS AND BOWS

"Arrows and Bows" uses palindromic and visual poetry to depict imaginary scenes of archery in medieval warfare. The first palindrome is a palindrome-by-letter and the second a palindrome-by-pairs. The third is palindromic by blocks of three letters (that is, "by-triples") and the fourth by blocks of four ("by-quartets"). Each palindrome is complemented by a glyphic visual work, illustrative of the palindrome's contents.

WARS OF ÞE ROSES AND ÞORNS

"Fog of War" is a bilingual palindrome whose first stanza is in English and whose second is in Welsh. "Niwl o Rhyfel" sees each stanza translated. This union of English and Welsh is followed by a statement regarding Richard III's death at the Battle of Bosworth Field (a battle won by Henry Tudor, thereby making him the only Welshman ever to claim the English throne). Here, it is revealed that the fatal blow to Richard III was most likely dealt by a popular fifteenth-century dagger that shares its name with a poetic form: the rondel. Accordingly, "Palindrome-Rondel for Richard þe Þird" is a rondel, palindromic and composed in iambic alexandrines. Moreover, in this rondel, the Old English letter þ ("thorn") is resurrected for the dual purposes of increased palindromic vocabulary and medieval affectation. This archaic letter is then used as the basis for two shorter poems: Firstly, a tautogrammatic octave, written in iambic tetrameter and loosely describing the events that took place during the Battle of Bosworth Field; and secondly, a poem of anagrammed lines, which obeys the medieval Welsh form "Englyn Penfyr" (a three-line poem, syllable count 10-7-7, whose second and third end-rhymes match the penultimate syllable of the first line, and whose first line's end-rhyme returns as the fourth syllable of line two).

<u>THE BODIES BELOW US</u>
"The Bodies Below Us" is a symmetrical visual poem made from Plate 214 of the *Codex Wallerstein* (1400s). The original image depicts a half-sword being thrust against a mordhau, in longsword combat. Both combatants are equipped with rondel daggers.

Five Romantics (in Firm Octaves)

<u>THE TEXTUAL POEMS</u>
"Idyll" features two ottave rime, one palindromic by letter and the other by pairs of letters. Each is composed in iambic tetrameter and in a style evocative of the Romantic Poets. It is followed by a sequence of five iambic triolets, written for five Romantics, in which each poem repeatedly anagrams a line from one of its subject's most famous poems. These are: "The nightmare Life-In-Death was she," (Coleridge, "The Rime of the Ancient Mariner", 1798); "I wandered lonely as a cloud" (Wordsworth, "I Wandered Lonely as a Cloud", 1807); "She walks in beauty, like the night" (Byron, "She Walks in Beauty", 1813); "'My name is Ozymandias, king of kings:" (Shelley, "Ozymandias", 1818); and "Fled is that music:—do I wake or sleep?" (Keats, "Ode to a Nightingale", 1819).

The section ends with a juvenile collage dedicated to two Romantic Poets, and featuring a typed, printed and glued palindromic poem in their honour. Also included are three pressed daffodils, contemporaneous sketches of the poets, drafts of "I Wandered Lonely as a Cloud" and "Kubla Khan", a detail from "A Field of Yellow Flowers" by Vincent van Gogh, and an illustration, by Gustave Doré, for "The Rime of the Ancient Mariner".

Prometheus Bound

THE TEXTUAL POEMS

The "Sonnets for Frankenstein" are Shakespearean in rhyme scheme and composed in iambic pentameter; the first is palindromic by letter, while the second has perfectly anagrammed lines. They discuss the events of Mary Shelley's novel.

Written for Herman Melville's *Moby-Dick*, "The White Whale" obeys a stricter combinatorial restriction: The first of the poems is a palindrome-by-letter, and the second is a palindrome-by-pairs. These two palindromes are perfect anagrams of each other.

Binding the previous poems, by conflating the novels to which they refer, "Prometheus and the Creature" studies *Frankenstein* and *Moby-Dick* as congruent tales of Promethean tragedy. The poem is in four terza rima tercets, all anagrams of each other.

THE RIGGING

Completing the suite, "The Rigging" features an abstract representation of the rigging typical of nineteenth-century whaling ships (many of which would later be repurposed for Arctic expeditions, such as Walton's). Below this shipless rigging is a tangle of lines, mimicking the ropes' reflection in water.

Observatory

"Observatory" begins with two constrained triads: "Orion" and "Boötes Void". Each triad features a poem of anagrammed lines, a palindrome-poem, and a perfect anagram of this palindrome. Next are "Remote Meteor" — a Petrarchan, monometer sonnet — and "Venus", a Shakespearean sonnet, in iambic dimeter, which uses every letter of the alphabet at least once. "Selene" and "Earth" resurrect the tripartite structure used for "Orion" and "Boötes Void"; in the case of "Earth", the palindrome is a palindrome-by-pairs.

GALILEAN MOONS
Prefaced by an anagram-poem of the style featured throughout this suite, the final piece makes concrete poetry from sketches by Galileo Galilei — specifically, Galileo's earliest drawings of the largest moons of Jupiter. (The sketches are believed to have been made during or shortly after the moons' discovery.)

The Piano

ROSE IDOL
"Rose Idol" presents a short palindrome, accompanied by three images of a piano, each in a different shade: greyscale red, black, and white. The piano depicted is a 1726 "Cristofori" (Bartolomeo Cristofori di Francesco is generally considered the inventor of the piano). The original sketch, taken from *Encyclopædia Britannica*, 11th ed., Vol. 21, p. 565, has been, in each case, recoloured and set against the decimal expansion of the twelfth root of two, as retyped on a restored antique typewriter.

"Red Piano" is a Shakespearean sonnet, in iambic pentameter, and an aelindrome in the twelfth root of 2 (which is the ratio of the frequencies of any two adjacent piano keys — that is, in any octave, the frequency of A multiplied by $^{12}\sqrt{2}$ gives the frequency of A#, and the frequency of A# multiplied by $^{12}\sqrt{2}$ gives the frequency of B, etc.). This aelindrome is taken to 47 significant figures (as detailed in its title).

BLACK PIANO

"Black Piano" is a musical aelindrome that parses beats, rather than letters, according to the decimal expansion of $^{12}\sqrt{2}$. The piece is intended for unaccompanied piano.

WHITE PIANO

"White Piano" is a visual aelindrome in the decimal expansion of $^{12}\sqrt{2}$, composed according to the same angular method as that employed in "Visual Aelindrome in e". This visual poem uses as its source image the opening two bars of Alexander Scriabin's Piano Sonata no. 7 — known also as "White Mass".

The Eureka Sonnets

"The Eureka Sonnets" studies six revolutionary thinkers from the worlds of literature and science: Edgar Allan Poe, Charles Darwin, Niels Bohr, Albert Einstein, Marie Curie, and Jorge Luis Borges. All six studies are Shakespearean sonnets, in iambic pentameter; two of the sonnets are palindromes-by-letter, while the others have anagrammed lines. The suite concludes with "Eureka", a monometer Petrarchan sonnet, complemented by concrete poetry made from Charles Darwin's most famous journal entry.

Passion and Permutation

"Passion and Permutation" begins with a simple anagram-poem: two six-line stanzas whose lines are perfect anagrams of the word "permutations". This is followed by a series of meditations on two of art's greatest inventors — Arnaut Daniel, who created the sestina fixed form, and Pablo Picasso, arguably the most prolific and celebrated visual artist of the twentieth century.

The premise of this section is that, in every work of art (and in every artist), there exists a negotiation between a calculating, structural idealism and a more explosive, expressive impulse. For Jorge Luis Borges, this complementarity was that of "algebra and fire". For Italo Calvino, it was "crystal and flame". In this suite of poems, the lives and works of Arnaut Daniel and Pablo Picasso are examined through the crystal lens of permutation and the creative flames of lustful passion.

Marked by their libidinous ways, both Daniel and Picasso wedded their creative ardour to an impersonal structural aesthetic: While Daniel arranged his poetry according to a cyclical interlocking of end words, Picasso portrayed his subjects and muses through the distanced, chrono-geometric permutability of multiperspectivism.

Accordingly, the poems of "Daniel and Picasso" discuss passion using structures that emphasise change within repetition. "Divine Comedy" finds Arnaut Daniel where Dante left him: suffering a cyclical penance in Purgatory, for his many lustful transgressions. The poem comprises six lines of anapaestic tetrameter, each featuring exactly six six-letter words. "Ardour Tiding" sees Picasso's eager creativity as a beach, recurrently cleansed by tides of passion

— reappearing the same, but changed. The poem is a palindrome-by-pairs whose shape traces the path of a shifting tide.

Next is "Anagram-Sestina for Pablo Picasso", which presents a critical analysis of Picasso's oeuvre, all the while cycling its end-words and permuting a fixed set of 36 letters. The poem is written in iambic pentameter, and its envoi employs the traditional word orders: 2-5, 4-3, and 6-1.

The final textual poem is both a sestina and a palindrome-by-letter. It follows Arnaut Daniel, wandering lost and recanting his lust, amidst fiery purgatorial mists — all the while singing about and within the cyclical form he invented. Rather than fighting them, the poem embraces the onerous trappings of its combinatorial constraint, to evoke the restriction, repetition, and tedious *drabness* of the once-passionate bard's purgatorial state. As with the preceding sestina, all lines are in iambic pentameter, and the envoi, which sees Daniel purged of his sins and finally in Heaven, obeys the word orders 2-5, 4-3, and 6-1.

CONCRETE SESTINA

The section concludes with a simple concrete poem, in which glyphic Arnaut Daniels are permuted, according to the pattern of the form he devised.

Mirror, Image

"Mirror, Image" features two iambic Shakespearean sonnets, each of which tangentially discusses, divided between its octave and its sestet, an optical instrument and a phenomenon involving reflection. The first sonnet, which addresses the camera obscura (octave) and the infinity mirror (sestet), is palindromic by letter. The second sonnet, whose subjects are the reflecting telescope (octave) and reflections in water (sestet), is palindromic by word. The two sonnets are perfect anagrams of each other.

As a complement to these anagrammed palindrome-sonnets, "The Shattered Mirror" presents an even more extreme experiment in palindrome-anagram combinatorial restriction: In this piece, the four subjects discussed in the preceding sonnets are re-examined within short, riddle-like palindromes of various styles: The camera obscura (top left) appears in a palindrome-by-letter; the infinity mirror (bottom left) in a palindrome-by-word. The reflecting telescope (top right) is addressed in a palindrome-by-pairs-of-words, while reflections in water (bottom right) are discussed within a palindrome-by-pairs-of-letters. All four palindromes are perfect anagrams of each other. Moreover, each of these palindromes is a perfect anagram of the introductory paragraph (very top of page 98).

OPTICKS

"Opticks" is a digital concrete poem that uses modelling software to map figures from *Cyclopaedia: or, An Universal Dictionary of Arts and Sciences* (Ephraim Chambers, 1728) onto human eyeballs.

Museum

SACRED WORLDS

"Museum" begins with two sonnets in iambic dimeter. The first has lines that are all perfect anagrams of its title; it discusses the legend of Atlantis. The second is a palindrome-by-letter, composed for the "Great Hymn to the Aten" (a poem-hymn written in fourteenth-century BC Egypt, for the sun-disk deity Aten, and traditionally attributed to the New Kingdom pharaoh Akhenaten). Each sonnet is joined by an ancient text that has been cropped, discoloured, desaturated and sharpened: "Atlantis Wished" features a distorted portion of the Gilgamesh cuneiform tablet on which the Great Flood myth is recorded. "Great Hymn to the Aten" features a rendering of Akhenaten's hymn (reworked from a drawing of the original, via N. de G. Davies, *The Rock Tombs of El Amarna*, part VI, "The Egypt Exploration Fund" (London, 1908)).

THE PRINTING PRESS

This poem-pair places a palindrome alongside concrete poetry made from desaturated text, abstracted from the *Gutenberg Bible* (the first major book to be printed in Europe using mass-produced movable metal type).

THE SOLILOQUY

"Halt Me" is a line-for-line perfect anagram of Hamlet's "To Be or Not to Be" soliloquy, as it appears in the *First Folio* (1623). The anagram takes direct inspiration from its source material's theme and poetic metre. (Note: all instances of f have been converted to s.) "Poor Yorick" is a distortion of a skull diagram by Leonardo da Vinci.

DISSECTIONS (OR, THE PEN AND THE SCALPEL)

"Dissections" presents an aelindrome in the decimal expansion of the plastic number (ρ). Accompanying this aelindrome is a visual poem depicting the repeated, rescaled "dissection" of a soft plastic surface, by a scalpel. The surface has been dissected according to aspect ratios of ρ^2 (which famously divides a square into three mutually non-congruent, similar rectangles).

THE ASTROLABE

In this piece, a triolet whose lines are perfect anagrams of each other is placed alongside visual poetry made from a diagram from the book *Compositio et operatio astrolabii* (a twelfth-century volume on the construction and operation of astrolabes).

THE CANDLE

"The Candle" features a palindrome that uses ampersands in place of the trigraph "and". This palindrome is then anagrammed, with the resulting anagram presented in an all-lowercase font that has been created specifically for this book.

SUNDIALS

The eight stanzas of "The Horizontal Dial" describe the confused shadows that form on a horizontal sundial, between dusk and dawn and through moonlight. The first stanza, also the last, is a palindrome-by-letter. The middle six stanzas are univocalic lipograms, whose single vowels appear in reverse alphabetical order. Complementing this horizontal sundial is concrete poetry made from a desaturated and sharpened photograph of the vertical sundial at Ely Cathedral, Cambridgeshire.

THE STRING SECTION

Here, a palindrome and anagram-poem "String Duet" meets a visual "String Quartet" made from Mozart's stave notation for "String Quartet No. 13 in D minor, K.173" and images sourced from *The Syntagma Musicum* by Michael Praetorius (1620).

SEISMOGRAPHY

"Seismography" begins with "Volcano", a palindrome-by-letter. To create "Seismograph", waveforms were generated by performing the palindrome on an acoustic guitar — with letters A to G played as their corresponding notes and letters H to Z left as pauses.

ENIGMA (FOR ALAN TURING)

Using the methods of its titular machine, "Enigma" generates a concrete poem from a palindrome-by-pairs, offering the latter as the "solution" to an encrypted text. Enigma machines encrypted messages through polyalphabetic encipherments: certain models, like the one replicated here, used a triadic encipherment, performed by a spindle with three rotors. Each rotor would be set to a specific starting position (a letter of the alphabet), the first of which provided a simple substitution cipher. A series of electrical plate contacts and pins would then communicate the message along the spindle, through the turning rotors, thus enciphering each letter two more times. To generate this poem's encrypted text (QZKME...), and in tribute to Alan Turing, whose wartime efforts helped crack the Enigma code, the three rotors' starting positions have here been set to Turing's initials: A, M, and T.

THE FEYNMAN DIAGRAM

"The Feynman Diagram" presents a diptych whose subject is Feynman and Wheeler's "One-Electron Universe" hypothesis. According to the hypothesis, the reason that all electrons possess exactly the same charge and mass is that there is, in fact, only one electron in the Universe, which has created its manifold incarnations by travelling both backwards and forwards in time — its backwards appearances being positrons. While the hypothesis was mostly meant in jest, in Feynman diagrams there is no clear distinction between electrons and backwards-travelling positrons. In honour of the purity and absurdity of this idea, "The Feynman Diagram" features both a Shakespearean sonnet, univocalic in e, and a whimsical Feynman diagram depicting a "cross-section" of such a world (complete with a quark-antiquark pair, materialising from electron-positron annihilation — a hint, perhaps, that *all matter* arises from this single, almighty electron...).

CHAOS THEORY

"Chaos Theory" begins with an aelindrome in the decimal expansion of Feigenbaum's First Constant (which describes the rate at which dynamical period-doubling bifurcation, and thus full chaotic behaviour, occurs). Although primarily inspired by mathematical and physical manifestations of chaotic behaviour, the poem also alludes to analogous theories of chaos in the fields of music and psychology. This textual poem is complemented by "Fractal Symmetries", which makes symmetrical concrete poetry from a simple, command-line depiction of the Mandelbrot set (the source image is a reproduction of the first ever recorded image of the Mandelbrot set — it has been taken from Wikipedia, where it is attributed to Elphaba).

Acknowledgements

Stray Arts (and Other Inventions) is the result of years of obsessive and often excruciating experimentation with the poetic potential of strict literary constraints. This book would not have been completed without the support and encouragement of many new friends in the poetry world and on social media. I would like to give special thanks to Christian Bök, for all the long conversations, and to Penn Jillette and Ian McMillan, for their generous support. Many thanks also to the following patrons and publishers: Pedro Poitevin, Lori Wike, Erica Castellanos, Lucy Dawkins, Ken Hunt, Derek Beaulieu, Gregory Betts, Merlina Acevedo, Craig Pepples, Rob McLennan, Petra Schulze-Wollgast, Joakim Norling, Michael Gardiner, and Philipp Blume. And thank you, Samuel Andreyev, for checking my notation for "Black Piano".

Most of all, I would like to thank my wife, Clara Daneri, to whom this book, and all my work, is dedicated.

Most of the poems in this collection have previously appeared else-where, either on Twitter, or in the following pamphlets, journals and anthologies:

PAMPHLETS FROM PENTERACT PRESS
"Ratio", "Matrix", and "Geometry" (as *Aelindromes* φ- π-√2, 2017)
"Prime Aelindromes" (2019)
"Palindrome-Rondel for Richard þe Þird"
        (as *Wars of þe Roses and Þorns*, 2016)
"Palindrome-Sestina for Arnaut Daniel" (2017)
"The Frankenstein Sonnets" (in *Poems for Frankenstein*, 2019)
"The White Whale" (2017)
"Red Piano" (2018)
"Mirror, Image" [without "Opticks"] (2017)
"Atlantis Wished" and "Great Hymn to the Aten"
        (as a leaflet pair, 2018)

PAMPHLETS FROM ELSEWHERE
"Lilith and Hecate", "Lilith and Pan",
"Lilith and Ra", and "Lilith and Hades"
        (as *The Lilith Sonnets*, No Press, 2018)
"Arrows and Bows" (Timglaset Editions, 2017)
"Anagram-Sestina for Pablo Picasso" (No Press, 2018)
"Five Romantics (in Firm Octaves)" [without "Idyll"]
        (No Press, 2017)
"Anagram-Sonnet for Jorge Luis Borges" (No Press, 2016)
"Selene" [parts two and three only] (Spacecraft Press, 2018)
"Halt Me" (Spacecraft Press, 2019)

PRINT JOURNALS AND ANTHOLOGIES

"Permutations" (*Concrete & Constraint*, Penteract Press, 2018)

"Famine Moon" (*Reflections*, Penteract Press, 2019)

"Palindrome-Sonnet" from "The Frankenstein Sonnets"
     (*Reflections*, Penteract Press, 2019)

"Anagram-Sonnet" from "The Frankenstein Sonnets"
     [early version] (*Touch the Donkey no.16*, 2018)

"The White Whale" (*Reflections*, Penteract Press, 2019)

"Eureka" (*ToCall no.3*, 2019)

"The Printing Press" (*ToCall no.1*, 2018)

"Volcano" (*Reflections*, Penteract Press, 2019)

"The Feynman Diagram"
     (*Concrete & Constraint*, Penteract Press, 2018)

ONLINE JOURNALS

"Iliad and Aeneid" (*Five2One Magazine*, 2016)

"Asymptote" (*Cordite Poetry Review*, 2017)

"Geometry" (*The Account Magazine*, 2016)

"For Wordsworth" (*The Wordsworth Trust*, 2016)

"Palindrome-Sonnet" from "The Frankenstein Sonnets"
     [early version] (*Eunoia Review*, 2017)

"Aelindrome in the Decimal Expansion of the Plastic Number"
     (*Burning House Press*, 2018)

"The Astrolabe" (*talking about strawberries all of the time*, 2018)

"The Horizontal Dial" (*Dusie*, 2018)

"Enigma (for Alan Turing)" (*Burning House Press*, 2019)

Anthony Etherin is an experimental formalist poet, a publisher, and a musician. He tweets poetry @Anthony_Etherin and archives his published works online at anthonyetherin.wordpress.com. He lives in the United Kingdom, on the border of England and Wales.

Reap and Sow

Repeat
its rite.
Recite
its beat:
The heat
whose light
invites
the wheat.
The rain
whose flood
converts
the grain.
The mud
and dirt....

THE
REAPING

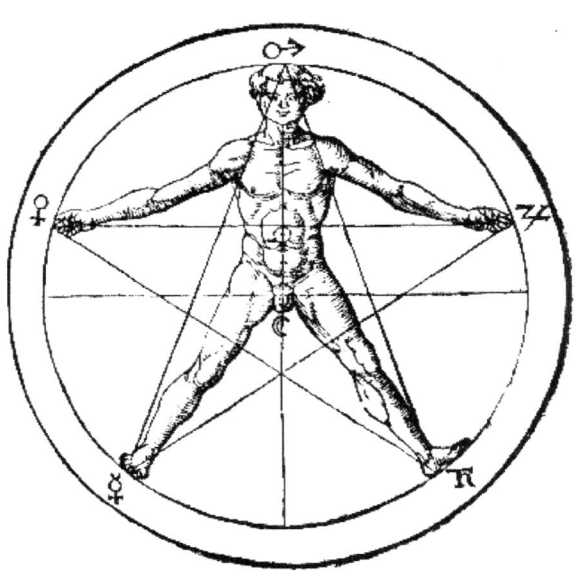

Laboratory

The Eureka Sonnets

Passion and Permutation

Mirror, Image

Museum

Weapons of War

Five Romantics (in Firm Octaves)

Prometheus Bound

Observatory

The Piano

The Reaping

Atoms, Gods and the Void

Sacred Numbers

The Lilith Sonnets

for Clara

Published by Penteract Press
PenteractPress.com
Twitter.com/PenteractPress

Copyright © Anthony Etherin, 2019

anthonyetherin.wordpress.com
Twitter.com/Anthony_Etherin

Designed by Anthony Etherin

Typeset in Minion

Printed by T. J. International Ltd,
Padstow, Cornwall

ISBN 978-1-9998702-6-3

FIRST EDITION

All images used as a basis for visual poetry are
either the author's own work or lie in the public domain

Collections by the same author:
Cellar (Penteract Press, 2018)
Danse Macabre (above/ground press, 2018)
Quartets (Penteract Press, 2019)
Otherworld (No Press, 2019)

STRAY ARTS
(and Other Inventions)

ANTHONY ETHERIN